# What My Mom Taught Me

## Camreon Dyer

What My Mom Taught Me

iUniverse books may be ordered through booksellers or by contacting:

iUniverse
1663 Liberty Drive
Bloomington, IN 47403
www.iuniverse.com
844-349-9409

Because of the dynamic nature of the Internet, any web addresses or links contained in this book may have changed since publication and may no longer be valid. The views expressed in this work are solely those of the author and do not necessarily reflect the views of the publisher, and the publisher hereby disclaims any responsibility for them.

Any people depicted in stock imagery provided by Getty Images are models, and such images are being used for illustrative purposes only.
Certain stock imagery © Getty Images.

ISBN: 978-1-6632-6906-5 (sc)
ISBN: 978-1-6632-6905-8 (hc)
ISBN: 978-1-6632-6904-1 (e)

Library of Congress Control Number: 2024924679

Print information available on the last page.

iUniverse rev. date: 12/04/2024

# What My Mom Taught Me

I dedicate this book to my daughter's Jaiyana and Macai; I hope that you BREATHE through life peacefully. And get all the things you dream with poise. Take what "I taught you" to the moon.

Love-Mommy

Today I got frustrated at school because I didn't get the grade I wanted on my quiz. I almost started to scream but then I smiled and remembered what my mom taught me.

1

Today at tennis practice, I had a really bad match. I didn't play as good as I expected.

I started to get mad but then I closed my eyes and remembered what my mom taught me.

Today I got into an argument with my classmate.
Because he said something really mean to me.
I wanted to hit him for saying what he said
but then I remembered what my mom
taught me.

Today I was at my grandma's house and she got really sick.
I got sad and started to cry but suddenly I smiled and
remembered what my mom taught me.

4

Okay, okay, I'm sure your wondering "What My Mom Taught Me"?

I know our Moms Teach us so many things that sometimes its hard to remember.

However, the one thing We do remember is our mom taught us how to breathe. Taking time to breathe is just as important as everything else.
Its how we function everyday.

She also taught me to read a book or practice yoga. My breathing is fun when I practice my handstand.

There is also and easier one where I do nothing at all but lay flat on the floor and breathe.

7

Did you know that sometimes one breathe isn't enough. If your feeling anxious take two quick breathes in and one out.

But the best part about breathing is that it can be done everywhere. But most importantly with your family in a quiet place.

8

My mom taught us that when things go wrong, just take a deep breath and calm yourself.

But the best part about breathing is that it can be done everywhere. So I never forget "What My Mom Taught Me".

# About the Book

This children's book is about a mothers lesson to her daughters about how to cope in stressful situations. If we teach our children the importance of Breathing and how it relaxes the nervous system then it will become natural to them as adults. Breathing is necessary and fun.

This book is filled with cool illustrations on different everyday life situations on how not to react first but to breath before reacting. Being suitable for boys, girls, toddlers, preschoolers and primary school students, this book is an excellent addition to a toolkit for parents, teachers and counselors.

# About the Author

Writer of Ten Poses of Yoga Memory Book, now a mother decided to take her knowledge to writing childrens books. Originally from Sacramento, CA, Camreon Dyer went to high school in Dallax, TX and graduated with a degree in Psychology from the University of New Orleans in neighboring Louisiana. Her eclectic work history, and ambitious nature motivated her to inspire others to pursue their dreams and especially children.